How to Survive a Breakup

An Essential Guide to Recovering from a Breakup, Getting over Your Ex, and Regaining Confidence

by Marco Cantoni

Table of Contents

Introduction

Breakups are probably some of the most perplexing yet most natural things in the world. People inevitably experience breakups as part of the process of finding the perfect partner in this very random world. And unless it's you plan to be single your whole life, you are going to come across people who you think will be with you forever, only to find later that that's not the case.

What makes breakups so unusual, however, is the fact that despite how normal and necessary they are, people tend to take them pretty hard. Even the emotionally strongest, most confident, and smartest of people feel tremendous pain, a sense of loss, and everything else in between, when what at one point seemed destined to be a long lasting relationship comes to an end.

It works both ways too. Whether you're the one finally calling it off, or you're the one caught like a deer in headlights with the unexpected talk of ending the relationship, both parties experience the same sense of loss. It's only natural, since you are letting go of something that changed your life one way or another.

But what you will notice is that some breakups go better than others. That is, though, in no way related how much the relationship meant to you or your partner. More often than not, how bad a breakup can feel depends largely on how well the entire process of breaking up is handled by both parties. It starts with the way one party decides to break it off, and how the other party receives the news. Of course the breakup also consists of the recovery period after the cutting of ties as well, including the process of coping and lasting right up until both parties are able to move on.

In an ideal world, breakups are supposed to help us grow and become better people, so that we not only prepare to enter into new relationships better suited for us, but we also avoid repeating the mistakes made in the past. Sadly, ours is far from being an ideal world, and not everyone who experiences a breakup ends up in such a positive state of mind. More often than not, people who were not ready to handle the loss end up feeling rejected and depressed, unable to function for an indefinite period of time. Others become obsessed with their ex-lovers to the point it becomes unhealthy for both parties. Still others end up losing their jobs, their friends, and even their self-respect. And sadly enough, worst of all, some people even commit suicide over a breakup.

None of those terrible things should ever happen to anyone, and they definitely don't need to happen to you. This book is designed to show you how you can be at your very best when the hard times come so that you are able to protect yourself from the worst effects of losing someone you have loved for a long time. It will take you through the entire breakup process, starting from the way you handle the actual breakup (as either party), to the way you will cope with depression, and finally to the point when you start to move on and find new relationships in the future.

Indeed, breakups can be a terrible experience, but they don't have to hurt as much as you might initially believe. With this guide, you'll learn how to make sure that your current (or next) breakup doesn't hurt you more than it should.

5

Chapter 1:   Breaking up with
Someone Else, Gently

Much like Tango, it takes two to break up—one to
decide to break the news and the other to take it all in
and decide what to do with the bomb that was just
dropped. Although there are times when a couple
mutually decides to end the relationship in a very
peaceful manner, it's very rare. More often than not,
the breakup is going to be unilateral on the part of
one and unexpected on the part of the other.

One important thing to remember is that breakups
will always be tough on both sides. Assuming that the
relationship was indeed genuine, the breakup would
be just as tough for the person bringing the news as
the one receiving it—only that the one who does the
breaking up is more prepared for the idea than the
one receiving the news. And as you go through
different relationships, you never can really tell if
you'll be the one breaking up with your partner or the
one getting the terrible surprise.

If you happen to be the person who finally decides to
end the relationship, you're probably the one who has
control over the entire situation. This means that you

have the most control over how the breakup will go and how bad the effects after breaking up can be. And if you're not careful, you could end up in much worse of a wreck than your partner. If you're unlucky enough, it could be your partner who will be wrecking you with his or her attempt to cope or get back at you for the terrible breakup.

So as the person who dumps someone else, you need to make sure that the relationship ends on civil, if not good terms, avoiding bad blood as much as possible.

Proper Timing

There's never really a "right time" to break up with someone, in a sense that, there's never a situation where everything will go as you would hope. But a lot of really terrible breakups that end bitterly are a result of poor timing. An utter disregard of when to break the news can severely make you lose control of the situation. You should definitely never break up with someone on a "date" or when your partner is in a bad mood. These poor choices of timing will only make you look deceptive and insensitive, and make him or her hate you more than necessary.

It's important to consider other factors, of course, but if you're already certain about the breakup, break the news as soon as possible. Chances are, it's already hard enough to decide to end the relationship now, and delaying the inevitable can only make letting go much harder as you and your partner continue investing in a relationship that's about to end. Find the best time to tell your partner, and do so at the earliest reasonable opportunity.

Secondly, you might want to bring it all down when you and your partner have time cope with both the short and long term effects of the breakup. If, for example, your partner is going through something that needs his or her full attention at the moment, breaking up with him or her right then and there could have terrible ramifications. On the short term, you also want to talk to your partner at a time when you both don't have to do anything else for the day, so both of you can have time to let it sink in.

Just like with all bad news, you want to be able to say it at the right time. A breakup shouldn't be treated any differently.

Proper Venue

Have you ever been to a restaurant where you, along with all the other people eating there, notice a couple in the corner, and one of them was crying loudly because they were breaking up? You don't want that. Just as important to right timing is finding the right place. Obviously, you need a place where both of you can talk, and there's room for both of you to do what you need to do in order to cope, and without affecting or having to be considerate of other people. Much worse than the awkwardness of the bad setting is the embarrassment that both of you could experience, which could make the breakup even more painful than it already is.

Experts say keep it private and in person. This is undoubtedly the most mature and most sensitive way to deliver the news of a breakup, allowing both of you equal opportunity to discuss the matter freely while keeping everything private between the two of you. You don't need the presence of passers-by with prying eyes. You can do it at your place or hers or even in a public place, as long as it's relatively private.

Do the breakup in person. The most cruel, insensitive, and dangerous way to break up with someone is to do it over the phone, social media, and worst, through text. Can you imagine how cruel it would be to treat the breakup like some memo where you say "oh, by the way, it's over" on an online messenger? That's just evil. Don't do that. Doing the breakup face to face is your chance to show concern and sincerity, proving that you took the relationship seriously and you did give this decision some thought.

If for some reason you're not comfortable with breaking up in a really private place, then make sure you choose a public place that doesn't have too many people. Remember that while this might make you comfortable at first, you run the risk of being embarrassed because your partner might make a scene.

Proper Explanation

Starting and ending relationships are the same in a sense that they are always about saying the right words. While nothing can ever be said to make your partner feel happy about breaking up with you, there are words that can show sensitivity and sincerity, which are much needed in times like these.

The first thing you need to remember is to keep things short and straight to the point. The biggest danger of breaking up is letting the discussion get out of hand, especially when emotions are starting to boil over. Of course, to balance things out, you need to explain clearly why you decided to let the relationship end. Don't leave your partner hanging with some vague message either.

As much as possible, avoid reciting a long list of things that you didn't like about your partner. No matter the reason for the breakup, playing the blame game is never a good way to justify your decision. You also have to be very honest, including important details that led you to the decision. For example, if it's because of someone else, then you have to say it. Your partner deserves to know.

Tip: A good rule of thumb as to what your partner should hear is to ask yourself what you would want to know if you were at the receiving end of the breakup instead.

Ultimately, however, you will have to accept that you can't completely convince your partner to break up with you. You're lucky if your future ex takes it gracefully. While you will want to listen to your partner's side, don't let it get to the point where you're just going in circles. Once you think everything that needs to be said has been said, it's time for you to walk away.

Chapter 2: How to Take the News of a Breakup

Although you know that your relationship is already on the rocks, you can never be truly ready for the thought of losing someone you've been with for a long time. Indeed, being at the receiving end of a breakup will always catch you off guard. Even people who claim to "see it coming", will still be hurt by the break-up.

But if your partner really wants out, there's really nothing you can do. Well, you can make it worse, but you don't want that. What you need to do when you're finally having "the talk" is to know how to handle the situation in such a way that you don't make it harder than it already is.

Now, you'll be lucky if the person you're dating is someone who is sensitive enough to do the things mentioned in the previous chapter to make the breakup easier, but not all lovers are created equal. However, should you also try to be as bad as the other party?

Keep Control of Your Reactions

Keeping your reactions under control doesn't mean that you should pretend to be okay. The news of the breakup will hurt, especially if you didn't see it coming, and you have every right to feel hurt. You, however, don't have the right to lose your cool, lash out, and mess up the discussion, much less make a scene.

Just like with any other situation where you receive terrible news or when you experience pain, you do what any other adult would do: manage the pain as you experience it. With breakups in particular, you need to understand that the decision was most likely just as difficult for your partner who decided to end of the relationship. By giving dignity to the fact that your partner was honest enough to confront you with his or her decision, you also give dignity to yourself.

You also don't have to say anything outright after receiving the news. In fact, you should compose yourself first so that you don't end up saying anything unnecessarily hurtful. Whether you're mad or you're sad, you need to be careful of what you say.

Say What You Need to Say, and Be Honest

As the person receiving the news, you're obviously not going to take this sitting down. If there's something that you think ought to be said, you should assert yourself (in a composed manner, of course). Breaking up is not just about the person initiating the conversation, after all. It's also about you, the person getting broken up with. Depending on how the conversation started, there are probably many things going on in your head. If there are things that you want to clarify, then you go ahead and ask.

Note: There are some people who are really vague about what they want to say, and sometimes you will have to be the one to ask if your partner is really breaking up with you. If your partner has not made it clear yet, then maybe you should ask what he really wants to happen with the relationship.

Go ahead and ask if you want to know why your partner is breaking up with you. Just make sure that you keep an open mind and be willing to accept the reasons as they are. Chances are, you're not going to be able to change his or her mind anymore. At that point, your goal should be to fully understand why your partner felt the relationship had to end.

There will definitely be things about the explanation that you might not completely agree with. But assuming that your partner has already made up his or her mind, you're going to want to respond to these concerns only to set the record straight. You can do this to figure out what you did wrong, or what changed during the time you've been together. You might also want to figure out if it's because of someone else.

Honesty here will be crucial. You need to clearly show to your partner if you're mad or confused because once you go your separate ways, there's a big chance you won't be seeing each other again for a long time. So if you want to say that the breakup is unfair or is based on shallow reasons, do so, keeping your emotions in check.

Note: Having a full-blown discussion about the breakup is not at all necessary. This depends on what your emotional needs are at the moment. If you think discussing the matter will help you cope in the future or at least help you get things off your chest, do so.

Do not, however, force yourself to engage with the situation. Don't ask questions if you feel you can't handle the answers.. While accepting the truth is important to coping with the breakup, it should come at the right time. In short, do what you think will help, and avoid the things you think will make things worse.

Again, don't ever try to change your partner's mind right then and there. You'll only end up going in circles, and that will repeatedly hurt both of you.

Avoid Spiteful Comments

If you're mad, don't use it as a license to say hurtful things to the person breaking up with you. Reciting a list of faults that you've always noticed about your partner in retaliation will not bring the relationship back. Badmouthing the other person that your partner is leaving you for is not going to convince him to get back with you, either.

Of course, this shouldn't stop you from rationalizing the breakup. If your partner is indeed making a mistake and is being unfair, then you need to remember that because it will help you get over the breakup easier. These thoughts, however, are not things you ought to slap in the face of the person who just broke up with you. Any kind of hostility, especially in public, is not going to help.

Just Say Goodbye

After all has been said, you need to exit the scene. The best way to do this is to just say goodbye. This is not the movies, where long lines are said before the breakup is consummated. You've already had your talk and you're not obligated to say anything more to the person who just broke up with you.

Attempting to cushion the conversation with words like "let's be friends," especially when it's not appropriate will only cause more pain. You've already been completely honest throughout the breakup, saying anything else just to save face is not going to do you any good. In fact, later on you'll learn that a complete cutting of ties and correspondence will be necessary as you try to mend your wounds, making it all the more important to avoid any pretentious feelings while the impact of the breakup is still fresh.

At this point, it's official. You've already broken up, and you need to get over your ex. You still have a long way to go before recovering from the loss, but if you handled the breakup well from the beginning, you would have made the coping process much easier than what most people end up having to go through.

Chapter 3: Opening up Your Breakup First Aid Kit

This is the part where you find yourself alone after walking away from the breakup. And the truth is, people find themselves in different states of mind at this point. It's almost impossible to tell you exactly what to do at the moment, because there will be a lot of things on your mind, and you're probably crying or angry depending on how you took the breakup.

But there are things that you need to make sure you do if you're going to survive this ordeal in the end. These are some of the things that you can do to help you cope with the initial shock of the breakup.

Take Care of Yourself

If you can, cancel all your plans, and go straight home. Most likely, you are in no condition to do or focus on anything at the moment, or the next day for that matter. Make sure you take a shower and get something to eat. These may seem like very trivial things now, (you just got broken up with, after all), but you'd be surprised at how inclined you'll be to forego a lot of these things while thinking about your ex-partner during the next few days.

Not taking care of yourself is not something you should be doing. In fact, you should be thinking a lot more about yourself at this point. That's why it's important to look after your immediate needs right now so you can pay attention to other things later. As the days pass, make sure you observe proper hygiene, get enough sleep, and have a healthy set of meals regularly. You can feel depressed but you shouldn't deprive your body of the proper care and nutrition it needs. This is not the time to get sick physically as you are already in a great deal of pain emotionally.

Let It Sink in

If you haven't done so yet, take time to come to terms with the fact that you're no longer going to see that someone you used to meet every day for what seems like a very long time. Sleep in, lounge around in your living room, and watch a movie while binging on your comfort food of choice if you must. Crying can even help.

Eventually you will pick yourself up and get back on your feet, but you need to give yourself time to accept this reality. If you go ahead and drown yourself in work or attend parties every other night, that piece of reality called breakup could catch you off-guard, hitting at the worst possible moment. You could end up bawling in public while you're drunk or trying to hide your sobs at the office. Let reality sink in, as it must, so you may as well let it happen sooner than later in a place you have total control of.

Erase Your Ex from Your Life

Once you're done crying, you're going to want to erase all traces of your ex. Here are a couple of things you'll want to do:

- Remove the things in your room or house that remind you of your ex. This includes photos, old gifts, and letters. Do whatever you want with them, as long as you get rid of these reminders. Some people, for example, like the feeling of burning those love letters. But if you can't find it in yourself to wreck every tangible piece of memory of your ex, you should at least put them away. Put everything in a box and hide them where you don't come across them.

- Delete those contact details. You may have memorized his or her phone number, but the fact that the contact isn't easily contactable through the phone book does wonders as an effective deterrent to any attempt to reconnect with the person.

- Do some cleaning on your social network. You don't want to end up getting notifications on your feed about your ex because you're not in the proper mental state to handle them. If you're not the type who burns bridges, you can make use of Facebook's hide function or temporarily block the person from Twitter. The goal is to make sure you don't accidentally get exposed to something about your ex on the internet when you're not ready. Certainly refrain from actively stalking the individual online.

Remember that you're not supposed to erase your ex's existence from your peripheral vision. You just need to establish a temporary environment where you can be isolated from him for a while. This is important so you can focus on yourself more while resisting any temptation to think about your ex.

While the tips mentioned above do not make a complete emergency medical service team, the first-aid measures you've read will keep you from jumping off the edge during the first few days. Keep nursing your heart to health for a day or two, and you're soon on your way to complete recovery.

Chapter 4: Keeping Negative Emotions Away

After you've erased traces of your ex from your surroundings, getting your mind off the breakup will be the next step to getting back on your feet. This will entail doing a bunch of things that will not only keep your mind off the breakup but be productive as well. To many, trying to get over a breakup is one of the times when productivity and creativity potential is highest. You've got all this unwanted energy—may it be sadness or anger—that you need to channel constructively somewhere. Here are a couple of things that you can do:

Spend time with friends and family. Not only is this one of the easiest things to do, it's one of the most rewarding as well. Here, you're not just trying to keep your mind off the relationship that you lost, but you're strengthening or rekindling old ones that you didn't have time for before.

It's great to be in the presence of family, especially your folks or siblings when you just experienced the worst rejection you've ever had in your life. Your family is that group of people who will never reject you. Families are never perfect, but everybody knows that no matter how bad the ties are, they'll always be there for each other.

Of course, your friends will be among the first people to hear about the breakup, and true friends will be there to pick you up when you're down. They'll remind you of the things you love to do and help you get your mind off the breakup. More importantly, they'll remind you about the best things about you and how lucky you still are despite all that's happened so far.

When spending time with loved ones, you don't really have to talk about the breakup. But if you feel that it will alleviate the pain, then your friends and family will be the best people to talk to.

Go on a trip. Some people need to go find themselves when they experience something terrible in their lives. This happens when they feel lost, not knowing what to do after all that's happened. Spending a few days (if not longer) in a place away from everything that's familiar gives you a fresh perspective of life. The distance allows you a bird's eye view of what you have going for you in life.

It might seem out of the way, even unplanned, but sometimes that itself is the beauty of traveling during such times. Take some time off and go out and explore the world. You will never know what you'll find out there but at the very least, you will find yourself.

Exercise. For those of you who don't really feel like doing anything drastic, working out or doing something physically challenging might prove perfect for mending the wounds of a breakup. Use all that pent up energy for something good for your body. Whether you're hitting the gym, running a few extra kilometers, or sitting on a yoga mat, breaking a sweat and building some muscle could be the key to becoming a much stronger person after a breakup.

Do something for others. Why not join a charity or simply do more acts of kindness to the people around you? Even science has shown that one of the best ways to find happiness is to make others happy. This is because it's very difficult to remain sad while doing something nice for someone, so undertaking this activity somewhat pushes you to find happiness inside of you.

Whether or not it helps make sense of your breakup, it does protect you from being drowned in what otherwise would be inexplicable sorrow. Breakups will make you feel like you've lost a lot of love, but when you choose to show love and kindness to others, you realize how much love you still have in you.

Chapter 5: What NOT to Do When Coping with a Breakup

Now that you know the dos of a breakup, it's time to learn the don'ts --what to avoid so as not to make things worse. A lot of the things that you shouldn't be doing might seem harmless at first, but they can really hurt you, especially when you're still in the process of trying to survive the breakup itself.

Many of these are pretty easy to avoid because they're primarily your own decisions, so it only takes awareness of what to not do:

Don't Overdo Anything. You'll be going through a lot to cope with the breakup. Whether it's going to a party, staying in to binge eat, or going on a vacation, make sure you don't do anything in excess. This includes not spending more than you can afford (not taking shopping or travelling to the extreme). The same holds true when it comes to drinking alcohol or drug use. Never allow a breakup to become a reason to put your health at risk. You are already mentally pre-occupied, don't add injuries and illness to the mix.

Sure, your friends and family will understand your need to be with them, but if you overstay to a point that you start to get in the way, it'll be unhealthy for all people involved. You also don't want to be away from school or work too much, because you might end up getting more stressed with the backlog. Remember that the point of surviving a breakup is to make sure you get back on track with your life—make sure you don't compromise all other aspects of your life while doing so.

Don't Try to Contact with Your Ex. While you may have done everything to cut off ties, the temptation will be there, and you might catch yourself trying unconventional methods to contact your ex. Now is not the right time for those "Hello's" and "How are you's." Your focus should be on yourself, so there's no need to see how your ex is doing.

Avoiding contact is important so you avoid comparing yourself with how your ex is doing. At this stage, you are in no condition to see your ex having the time of his life, possibly with someone new. Everybody deals with pain at a different pace, and you shouldn't give yourself reason to think that your recovery is slower than your ex's.

Don't Say Bad Things About Your Ex. If you must discuss the circumstances of your breakup with other people for whatever reason, you should never badmouth the other person. This applies regardless of how the relationship ended. Keep any bitterness to yourself. If your ex says bad stuff about you, be the better person and don't start hating other people just to make yourself feel better. After all, there was a time when you did love that person.

You'll surely be tempted to do any of the things mentioned above and more. When sorely tempted, do the right thing and just say no for you're doing this not for anyone else but yourself.

Conclusion

Stop spending your days blaming yourself, wallowing in self-pity within the confines of your own bedroom, or worse, trying to get back with your ex. It's heartbreaking, but losing someone who you thought was important to you is not the end of the world. Just like with any other tragic experience, you are expected to rise above the sadness and come out a better person. This is life—breakups will happen and you must move on. It may take a while but things will get better.

And if you are one of those who survived the storm, make sure you use this newfound awareness to help others get over their own breakups. . Help them see that this is only, at worst, the end of a relationship, but never the end of life itself. Most importantly, you need to help them realize that no matter how much it hurts, everything is going to be okay.

Finally, I'd like to thank you for purchasing this book! If you found it helpful, I'd greatly appreciate it if you'd take a moment to leave a review on Amazon. Thank you!

Made in the USA
Lexington, KY
27 October 2018